First Published March 2026
ISBN: 979-8-9868445-3-4

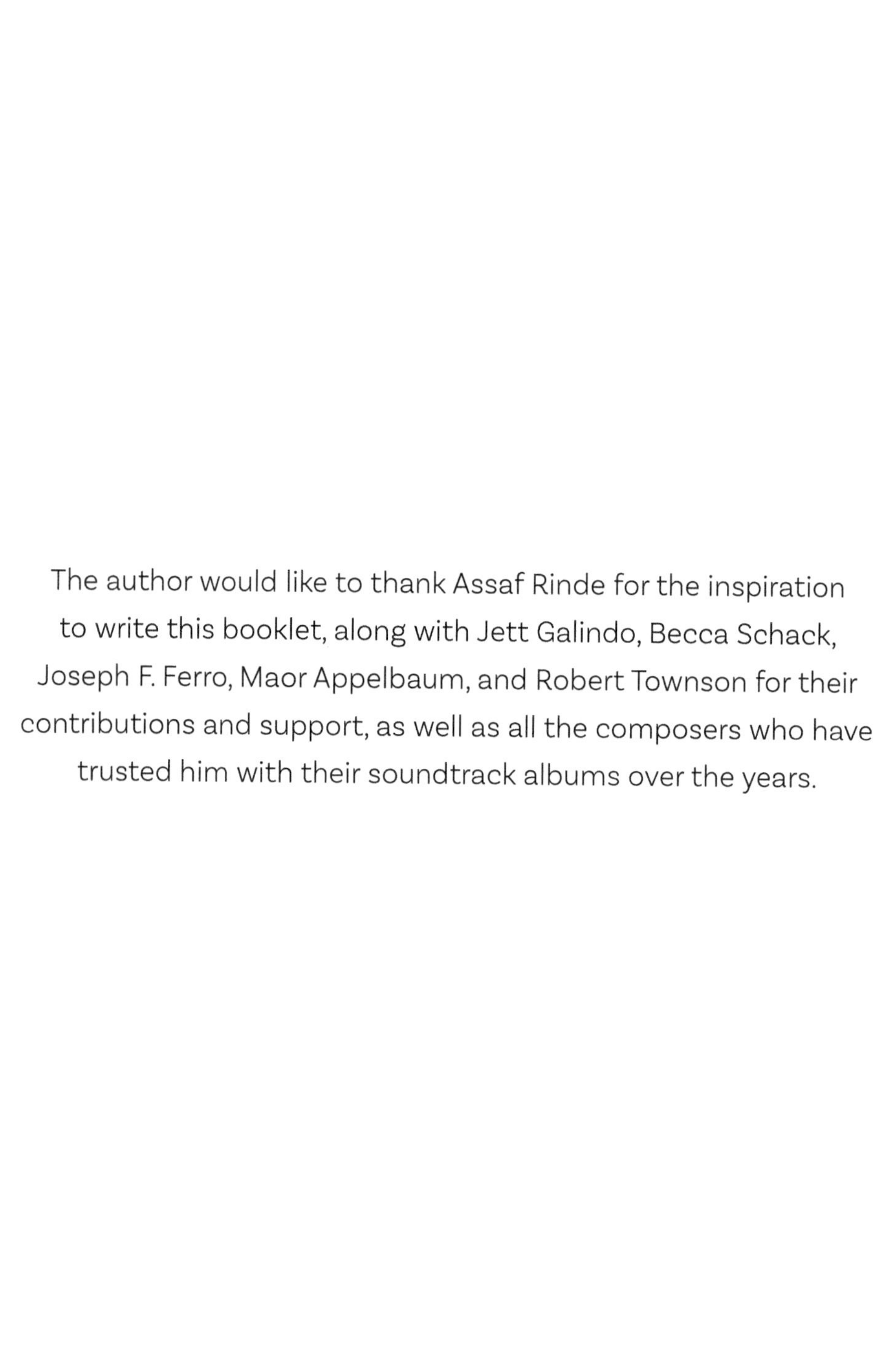

The author would like to thank Assaf Rinde for the inspiration to write this booklet, along with Jett Galindo, Becca Schack, Joseph F. Ferro, Maor Appelbaum, and Robert Townson for their contributions and support, as well as all the composers who have trusted him with their soundtrack albums over the years.

Table of Contents

Foreword

by Robert Townson

In a lifetime dedicated to the production of soundtrack albums, I've often reflected on how truly unique this artform is—bridging the worlds of film and music, storytelling and listening. Over the course of my career, I've had the profound privilege of producing almost 1,500 albums, including collaborations with composers ranging from Jerry Goldsmith and Elmer Bernstein to Alex North and Hans Zimmer. Each album has been its own journey, a new puzzle to solve. And yet, no matter how many times I've done it, the process of shaping a dramatic score into a compelling and satisfying album remains as complex—and as rewarding—as ever.

Shie Rozow's The Art and Craft of Creating Engaging

The Art and Craft of Creating Engaging Soundtrack Albums

Soundtrack Albums is a rare and welcome deep dive into this very process. With clarity, warmth, and great respect for the material, Shie breaks down the often-invisible decisions that go into crafting a successful listening experience from music originally written to support on-screen storytelling. His willingness to pull back the curtain on the editorial decisions—what stays, what goes, what is trimmed or combined—is invaluable for composers, editors, producers, and fans alike. Most importantly, his love for the music and his desire to present it in the best light come through on every page.

This book does not claim to offer the only way to approach soundtrack album production—and that's part of what makes it so honest. There is no single formula. In truth, every project is different. The needs of an intimate indie drama differ wildly from those of a large-scale franchise, just as a richly thematic symphonic score requires a different touch than a sparse, textural one. There are choices—endless ones—and even among seasoned producers, opinions and methods vary. Some albums benefit from preserving the full score in film order (though, in my opinion, very few do), while others demand a radical reshaping to become something cohesive and musically satisfying on their own. That creative balancing act is what makes this such a fascinating, ever-evolving craft.

In my case, my album output has also included a huge number of film music releases that are not soundtrack albums, but rather new recording projects—often with orchestras, big bands, jazz ensembles, or intimate chamber groups—where so many decisions have to be made before a single note is ever played. But that opens a whole other can of worms, rich with its own creative challenges and rewards.

My history of album sequencing and production has also greatly informed how I design and put together new concert programs. The skills involved in shaping a satisfying listening journey—whether on an album or in a concert hall—are deeply connected. So the experience of album sequencing can absolutely pay off in other ways, far beyond the studio.

I'm deeply grateful to Shie for taking the time to articulate these nuances so thoughtfully. He brings not only his own significant experience to bear, but also a generosity in sharing the behind-the-scenes thinking that most of us simply learn on the job. In doing so, he is helping to elevate the conversation about how scores live beyond their films, and how soundtrack albums can serve as artforms in their own right.

If you care about film music—as a composer, a producer, or simply as a listener—there is much here to savor. As someone who has devoted a life to these albums, I welcome this book with open arms and celebrate the spotlight it places on a discipline that is so often overlooked, but never less than essential.

- 4 -

Introduction

The art and craft of film scoring is a form of storytelling. The score is designed to complement what we see on the screen. It can sever a myriad functions in countless ways that will affect the way the viewer experiences the story. Ultimately the music is there to fulfill a supportive role, it is not the star. This doesn't mean film/TV/videogame music can't be exquisite and engaging on its own, but none of it would be written as it was if it wasn't for the scene(s) it accompanies.

When listening to an album, the music is the star. The whole point of an album is to listen to the music on its own. It's music for the sake of music. Whether we're listening to songs or instrumental music, no matter the genre, an album is designed to stand on its own. It's not usually created for any other purpose other than the pure enjoyment of the artform. Yet when it comes to soundtracks, we find ourselves in the unique position of needing to find a way to make music that wasn't originally designed to stand on its own shine and be the star it was never designed to be.

I've had the privilege of creating more than 50 soundtrack albums for composers including Danny Elfman, Pinar Toprak, John Ottman, Deborah Lurie and others, and have learned a thing or two about what makes a good listening experience in the process. Like most things, there is no one way to do anything. Others may have different approaches to doing this or may disagree with some or all my recommendations here, and that's OK. This short booklet will guide you through my approach to creating engaging soundtrack albums that offer enjoyable listening experiences and present the score in the best possible light based on my experience.

Part One
Organization

Like all aspects of film scoring and music making, keeping organized is key. It's quite common to go through several iterations of a soundtrack before finalizing it, so keeping track of all your assets and versions and variations is key. This is particularly true when you're creating a soundtrack for a client rather than yourself.

The first thing I do when creating a soundtrack album is create a new Pro Tools session and import the mix of every single cue from the project into this session. You don't have to use Pro Tools, you can do this in any DAW, though Pro Tools is an industry standard for music editing, and in my experience most (though not all) mastering facilities or independent mastering engineers will be very happy to receive a Pro Tools session and will likely do their work in that DAW.

Clearly name the session with the name of the project — I like to add "Soundtrack" and a version number. Every time I make any adjustments to the soundtrack album, I'll first do a save-as of the session and increment the version number. For example, if I'm creating a soundtrack for a film called My Awesome Movie I'll name my session "My Awesome Movie Soundtrack v1" then as I make adjustments to the album, subsequent sessions will be named "My Awesome Movie Soundtrack v2," etc.

When importing the tracks, I typically only use the stereo mixes, not stems. I make sure to import every single cue, including very short cues that would never stand on their own, alternate versions, and even cues that didn't make it into the production. I want to have easy access to all the music that was created for the project as my starting point.

Sometimes it might be useful to import the full set of mix stems to create some very creative music edits. In my experience, this is the exception and may only be needed for just one or two cues, so I always start with just the stereo mixes, and if I find I need stems, I'll import those for the cues that require them. For example, when I worked with Danny Elfman on Spider-Man 2, there were two soundtrack albums released. One was Spider-Man 2: Music from and inspired by and the other was Spider-Man 2: Original Motion Picture Score. The former album consisted mostly of songs, with 2 score suites that we created specifically for this album. The suites combined music from several cues and were heavily edited requiring stems to successfully achieve what we were after. They simply wouldn't have been possible using just the stereo mixes.

Another example can be heard on the soundtrack to Charlie and the Chocolate Factory, another collaboration with Danny Elfman. There is a track called "The Boat Arrives" that is based on a cue by the same name. However, the cue in the film was quite a bit shorter than the album version. Danny wanted to expand it for the soundtrack. By using the stems, we were able to create an extended, gradually building introduction to the cue. We started with some of the percussion stems, then looped them, and added other percussive stems. Then we brought in vocal stems and eventually we got to where the orchestra joined, at which point the cue plays as originally written to picture. This made for a much more engaging and interesting cue for listening purposes. If memory serves, that was the only track where we used stems on that album.

Another reason to using stems instead of stereo mixes is If the soundtrack is to be released in surround sound, or ATMOS or any other immersive format you'll either need to provide stems, or the full mixes in the desired format.

Sometimes you may want to rebalance or remix a cue for soundtrack purposes. When mixing for film/TV we must consider dialog and sound effects, so there may be musical elements that could easily be featured that aren't in the film mix so they don't compete with dialog or effects. We can use the stems to rebalance the stems or even do a remix of a cue so that such elements can be more featured in the album version. A common example is the use of bell-type sounds like celesta or glockenspiel, or soloists. I've seen composers remix cues to bring those out more in the album version than in the film version.

Keep in mind that the mix stems are often not stereo mixes but are in a wider format including LCR, Quad, 5.1, 7.1.2, etc. Unless I'm creating a 5.1 or ATMOS soundtrack album, which is quite unusual, when the edit is done it will have to be converted to a stereo mix for the album. This is called folding down or bouncing to a stereo file. In such cases I always check with the scoring mixer as to his/her settings when folding down from the wide format to a stereo mix and match them. Usually it's easy to duplicate, lowering certain channels by specified amounts. But on occasion the mixer might use certain plug-ins or outboard gear that I don't have to achieve this. If this is the case, I'll send him/her my edited track as a Pro Tools session and ask them to run it through their audio chain to fold it down to a stereo mix. This ensures that the result sounds exactly as intended and I'm not accidentally changing the balance of anything by folding it down differently than intended.

Whether I'm only using stereo mixes or stems, keeping my session well organized and having all the cues available at my fingertips is extremely helpful. I like to line them all up back-to-back in score order, so I have an easy visual of everything as my starting point.

Below is what that looks like using stereo mixes.

- 12 -

Part Two
Trim the Fat

Now that I have my session set-up and all the tracks are readily available, I like to go through everything and do what I call "trim the fat." What I mean by this is getting rid of any unnecessary bits that may have been needed to properly fit the scene or for other technical reasons but aren't necessary for a pure musical experience.

First, I go through all the cues and simply trim the silence at the beginning of each cue. I like to leave anywhere from 1 to 6 frames of silence before the audio begins – usually it's just a frame or two for music that has a very hard start, like action or percussive cues, and a bit more for softer cues that sneak in. That way if the listener jumps from track to track there's the tiniest of gaps to ensure the beginning doesn't get clipped if there is any sort of automatic fade in or glitches, but there also isn't an awkward pause before the music plays. As you can see in the image below, there is now empty space after all the (tracks on the right), equaling the amount of silence I trimmed from all the beginning of all the cues. This gives me a more realistic idea of how much music I have to work with. In this example a little over 46 minutes.

Next, I duplicate this track and rename it "All trimmed". From here on, all the work is done on the duplicate track. The original track remains untouched. That way if I ever need to go back to an original unedited cue, I have it readily available and trimmed.

I listen to every cue and look out for unusual meters that wouldn't occur had the music not been designed to fit picture. For example, if we're in a 4/4 groove and there's a single 5/4 measure, which was obviously created to extend the music to hit a specific moment in the picture, I'll most likely cut 1 beat out of that 5/4 bar to keep the groove steady. However, just because there is an odd meter here or there doesn't mean it has to be changed. It's very common to have odd meters within music for the screen. What we're listening for are things that stick out, that catch our ears when consumed without the picture they were written to. In some instances, I may do the reverse and add a beat or an 1/8th note to a bar if that makes it sound better as a pure listening experience. If I feel anything bumps me, I address it.

At the same time, I listen for music that sounds too repetitive. It's not unusual in film-scoring to sometimes vamp until it's time for the next change in the music. Sometimes it's under dialog, or we're simply continuing the energy under an action sequence, but when listening to the music on its own it can become repetitive, going on for too long, which makes it not very engaging after a while. If I feel this is happening, I'll trim some of these repetitions. Oftentimes this can happen during a buildup to a big shift in the music. For example, this could be a chase scene building to a crash or explosion. Here, the music might have some kind of underlying loop with a slow build on top that can take quite a while to reach its apex. In the context of the film, the slow increase in tension and excitement works incredibly well, but on its own, as a listening experience, it could feel like we're gilding the lily, and it just goes on a bit too long. If that's the case, I'll shorten such a buildup to what feels more natural without having the visuals to support it.

Another common thing I'll find is held notes that hold for a long time. These often occur at the beginning of cues, which sneak in at a particular key moment in a scene, and just hold until there is reason for the rest of the music to kick in. Or sometimes, especially in horror films, there is some sort of musical effect or musical sound design that creates wonderful tension as something is slowly unfolding on the screen. But without the picture, listening to a long held-note or musical effect for too long can become boring, so I'll shorten those.

I've found that in some scores, especially comedies, there can be parts of a cue that are practically copy/pasted from another cue, and other parts that are different and fresh. In those cases, I'll cut out the bits that feel like we've heard them before in other cues that aren't necessary and only use the part of the cue that is unique.

If there's a lot of silence after the cue ends, I'll usually trim that and add a fade out to the end of the cue, to make sure there are no accidental ticks or pops at the end of each cue.

Once I've "trimmed the fat" my session will look something like the image below. As you can see compared to the previous image, there is even more empty space after all the cues, which corresponds to the duration of everything I trimmed so far. In this example the total duration is now around 38 minutes.

Below is a closeup view of one of the tracks I trimmed. I left the original right above the trimmed version to make the difference visually clear. As you can see the one on "All Trimmed" track has had the silence in the beginning trimmed, as well as some rests significantly shortened.

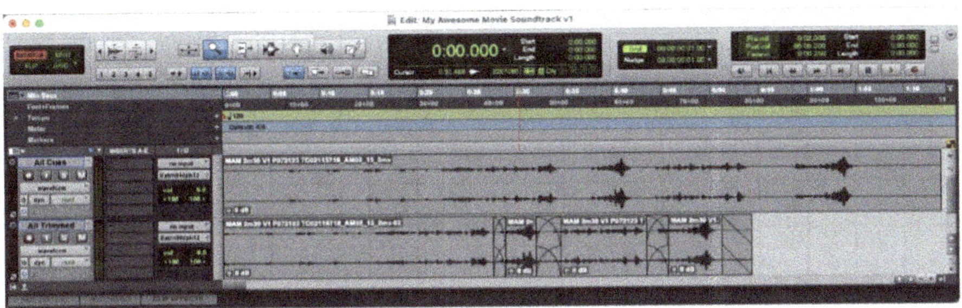

Once I'm done with this pass, I identify cues that are reiterations of themes or ideas in a similar fashion. Themes and variations are great and work very well both within the context of a film, TV show or video game and in a soundtrack album. But sometimes a second or third iteration of a theme might be very similar to a previous one, especially when working on a TV series. It's not uncommon to essentially copy/paste a theme into a different scene in a different episode and then simply adjust to it to fit that scene. This works well in this context, but as an album listening experience it can sound repetitive. If I find these types of cues, I pick the one that's the most complete iteration of the theme (usually the longest version) and mute the others.

I also look out for particularly short cues that don't feel particularly strong on their own and mute those, too. These are most commonly found in comedy scores, where we may have very short cues to accentuate a joke, or sometimes we have stingers in horror movies that are essentially a brief musical effect. They play a crucial role within the context of the project, but on their own they aren't especially memorable or compelling. That said, if I'm particularly fond of a short cue, I'll try to find a way to combine it with other cues so it can be included within the context of a longer track. More on that in the next chapter.

Here's an image of what my session looks like once I'm done with this pass. As you can see there are several muted clips within the string of cues.

Finally, once I'm done with all the above, I tend to move all the muted cues to the end of my session, so I'll have all my usable cues back-to-back followed by my rejected cues. This way I still have everything, but it's been optimized and organized so I'm ready to move on to the next step, which I discuss in the next chapter. As you can see, this is practically identical to the image above, but all the muted cues are now at the end instead of being interspersed throughout. This also helps me see that I now have about 33 minutes of music available for this album.

Below is a screenshot with all the steps described in Parts 1 & 2 and the examples provided look like if shown together. I think this helps visualize where I start, and where I end up when preparing the materials for an album. It gives me a very clear indication of which cues are in play for inclusion in the album, and what the total duration of all those cues is. Now that all these steps are done, I have a great starting point for the more creative part of the process, which I describe in Part Four: Sequencing of this booklet.

Part Three
Album Duration

Once I'm done organizing all my cues and trimming everything that I think is superfluous, it's time to make some technical and creative choices. The first question that comes to mind is how long we want the album to be. There are a few considerations to keep in mind when determining the duration of an album.

First, the style of the music. For example, a beautiful, melodic, sweeping score with many variations including epic, dramatic, action and emotional cues can carry a listener for quite a while. Conversely, a dark, atonal, tense score that is non-melodic and doesn't have as much stylistic variety might overstay its welcome as a pure listening experience sooner than the former example. These are entirely subjective considerations, and hardcore score fans will want the most complete and unaltered versions of any soundtrack they can find but try to consider how the average listener will experience the album when deciding on length. Sometimes I don't have a specific duration in mind, and I just discover what it will be when I finish creating the album.

Second, consider the type of score it is. Is this album the soundtrack to a movie? A limited series? An episodic series? A video game? Whittling down a score that was originally several hours long (say for a video game or series) to fit in an album will leave out quite a lot of music and may deprives the audience of a lot of material. In such a case a longer album may be appropriate to squeeze in as much music as possible. Conversely, whittling down a 50- or 60-minute score to 45-50 minutes is much easier and will leave out very little. If the score is particularly short, it may not warrant a soundtrack album, or if you do choose to release one, it might be an EP.

Third, consider the medium in which you are releasing the album. A CD can hold a maximum of 80 minutes of music, though it's good practice not to go beyond 74 minutes for a variety of technical reasons. If you're creating a digital only release, most distributors will allow you up to about 2 hours per album. However, if you're planning on a vinyl release you have very real physical limitation of about 20-25 minutes per side depending on the music (more on vinyl later). If you have a particularly long score and plan on a vinyl release, consider a double album.

When I was tasked with creating a soundtrack album for

coming in at 1 hr. 59 min. For the double vinyl album, the duration is about 79 minutes, a full 40 minutes shorter than the digital version. This forced us to make many difficult choices in terms of what to include, what to exclude and the order in which we would sequence the tracks.

Fourth, if the score was recorded under a union contract, there may be financial implications regarding the duration of the album. I'm not up to speed on the current contracts of the American Federation of Musicians (AFM), but I remember in years past having to limit albums that were recorded using AFM contract to either 45 or 60 minutes. It's always good to check if there are any such considerations that must be taken into account based on where the score was recorded and under what type of contract.

Fifth, will the soundtrack include songs? If so, how many? Sometimes a soundtrack album can include mostly songs and just one or two score suites as is the case in Spider-Man 2: Music from and inspired by, which I described earlier. In that case the score was limited to 2 tracks, each limited to 4 minutes or less. The rest of the album was made up of songs. In the case of Guardians of the Galaxy, there were several soundtracks issued. There was Guardians of the Galaxy: Awesome Mix Vol. 1, which included twelve songs from the film and none of the score; Guardians of the Galaxy: Original Score, which included twenty tracks of Tyler Bates' score; and finally Guardians of the Galaxy Deluxe, a double album that combined both previous albums. However, the vinyl version of the score only includes 16 tracks due to limitations I touched on briefly and will discuss at more depth in Addendum: Vinyl Albums at the end of this booklet.

As you can see there are all sorts of considerations that go into how long an album should be — ranging from technical, to financial, to purely creative. These questions must be answered before proceeding to prepare the score for an album release as they will affect the creative choices that will be made, including what music to include, what to omit, and/or how to edit cues for the best possible presentation within the context of the type of album that is to be released.

Part Four
Sequencing

Now that we have an idea of how long we want our album to be it's time to consider the sequencing of the tracks on the album. This is the most creative parts of the process, where we make choices about which tracks to include, which to exclude, combine cues into single tracks, make creative editorial choices, and decide on the order of the tracks.

The first thing I do is create some work tracks. I'll usually add a pair of tracks and label them "MX A" and "MX B" so I can checker-board tracks or easily make edits involving overlapping cues. Sometimes I might need more tracks if I want to overlay something, so I can add a "MX C" track, etc. When working with stereo mixes a pair of stereo tracks is usually all I need. When working with stems, I might create two sets of tracks corresponding to the stems I have and add "A" and "B" to the track names, so I have an "A" set of stems and a "B" set of stems. I then group each set of stems so by default when I edit them, they are all kept together. I can ungroup them for intricate editing involving the stems when I work on those cues.

At this point it's time to choose the trimmed cues that will definitely go into the soundtrack album and move them down to the "MX A" track. I like to keep them all lined up back-to-back (See image below). I then check the duration of the album. If it's shorter than I'd like, I now have choices to make about which unused cues I want to add. This is a wonderful problem to have. I find that adding more material is fun and it feels good to be able to include more music. However, if it's too long, I must make choices about which of my chosen cues have to be eliminated from the album.

If I'm adding more cues, I consider which cues I think will add the most variety and interest to the album as a pure listening experience. Most scores tend to lean in a certain direction based on the genre of film/TV show/Videogame they are scoring. A dramatic film will have lots of dramatic cues, so I might try to find some lighter cues if they exist. A romantic comedy will tend to have lighter and comedic cues, so I might look for some more emotional cues or dramatic cues if they exist. An action film will have lots of action cues, so I might look for more dramatic or lighthearted cues if they exist. The point is that if a score leans heavily in a certain style/genre, listening to track after track that are in that same world can make for a monotonous listening experience. Therefore, interspersing other cues throughout helps make for a more engaging listening experience.

If I have too many cues and need to remove some, I use the same approach but in reverse. I try to identify which types of cues I have the most of, and I'll most likely get rid of one or two of those types of cues so that the album has good variety.

At this point I look at the duration of each cue and identify shorter cues that might be combined to create longer tracks. It's quite common to have short cues in a score (I'd say under 2 minutes is short), yet I find that albums with lots of short cues aren't as fun or engaging to listen to as ones with tracks that are longer. This is especially true when there are a lot of cues that are just a minute or so long, or even shorter. Albums with lots of short cues like that feel very choppy to me. Therefore, I always look for opportunities to combine cues that naturally segue from one to the next to create a longer piece of music that is interesting and engaging. If I have cues that were designed to segue from one to the other in the first place to form a continuous piece of score, I'll start by recreating those segues to create longer continuous tracks for the album.

Next, I'll find the shorter cues that are still available and see if any can be combined in an elegant and seamless way to create longer tracks. When doing this I don't hesitate to combine cues that might have been far apart within the production. If it sounds good, I'll gladly combine a cue that came from reel 1 and a cue that came from reel 7 into a single album track. Here's what that might look like. In the following example, track 6 is made up of 1m19, 1m18 ALT & 2m38 ALT.

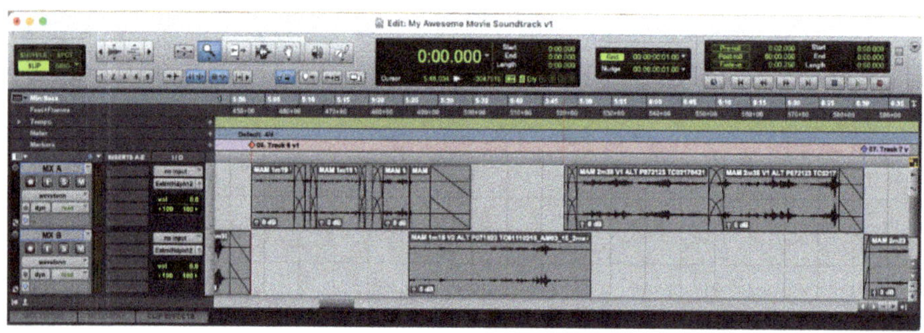

It's not uncommon to be able to combine different cues together in different ways. For example, 6m48 might segue beautifully both into 2m08 and into 4m32. Or 4m32 might work just as well on either side of 6m48. In those cases, I keep the different combinations as options to consider when sequencing the album. These options might work differently in context depending on where in the album they appear. So, I'll create all three versions - 6m48 segueing into 2m08, 6m48 segueing into 4m32 and 4m32 segueing into 6m48. Then I can decide which one to use and where in within the album later by trying different possibilities.

Now that I have all these tracks, it's time to figure out their order and make decisions about which ones make it into the album and which don't. In my view the job of a soundtrack album is not just to highlight the music on its own, but also to evoke the story of the film/TV show/videogame it came from. It reminds the listener of that story. Therefore, I start out by keeping things in the order in which they appeared in the film. This is the most accurate linear and musical representation of the story. Then I go to the beginning and play through and listen.

As long as I feel engaged and am enjoying the album I see no need to change anything. But often within a few tracks I feel like I'm ready for some variety that isn't there yet. This makes sense, stories are usually told in 3 acts and tend to lead up to a climax with a few ups and downs on the way. The first act typically has an introduction or exposition, followed by an ignition point that sets up the story to follow. The second act typically unfolds the story/action and builds on the story. The third and final act leads up to the climax, which is the culmination of the story. If the 3-act structure were a graph, I think it would generally be a mostly linear rising graph.

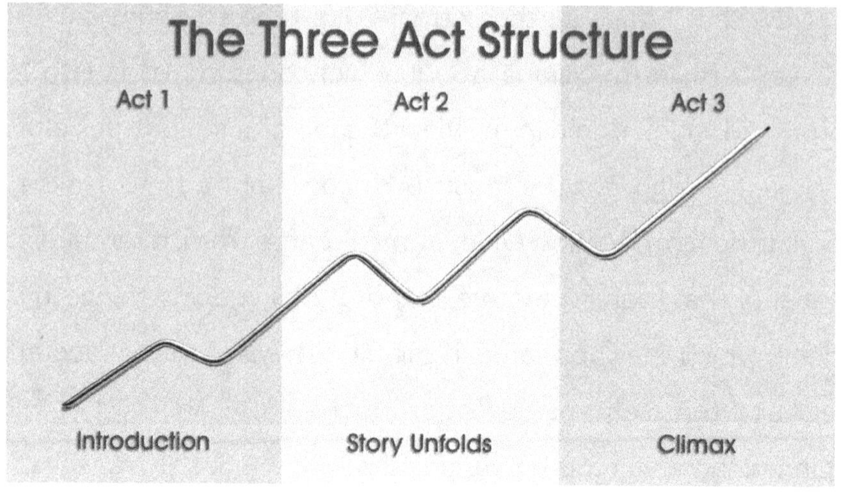

Therefore, the early cues in a film might have a similar intensity that helps the setup, the middle cues will usually have a bit more variety and the latter cues build to the climax and help elevate that apex of the film. This works great when telling a story, and has some ups and downs, but might not work as well as a listening experience. I approach a soundtrack album more like a roller coaster ride, making sure there are lots of ups, downs and turns to keep the listener engaged. This is true even for a very mellow score say for a romantic film, I still try to create the most engaging sequence I can that makes the most of the material available.

If I feel there isn't enough variety, I'll find a later cue from the film and move it up in the album sequence to create some contrast with the surrounding cues. I keep listening and repeat this process until I feel I have a good sequence, trying out different ideas and options until I'm happy. Then I go back and listen again from the top to make sure it's working well. Sometimes it does at which point there's my first pass of the album. But sometimes, I find that this first attempt ends up being a bit uneven — at least half the time in my case. If I have options of combo cues, as described above, I'll create an alternative sequence and listen to see which I prefer. Typically, I listen at least 3 or 4 times and make tweaks, moving tracks around, trying different cues in different locations, or even experimenting with which tracks to include or exclude before I'm satisfied.

Once I'm satisfied, I'll jump around to about 10-15 seconds before the end of each track and listen through to the next track. What I'm listening for is the spacing between the tracks. There is no standard, no right or wrong answer as to how much space there should be. I set the spacing purely on instinct. I listen to the transition and it either feels like the next track will come in early, late or just right. If it's early or late, I'll nudge it to adjust the spacing until I find that moment that feels just right. I repeat this process for every track on the album.

Once that's done, I like to add markers to indicate the beginning of each track, which I name with the track number and name. Depending on the client and circumstance I'll either just give each track a name (usually matching the cue name, though not always), or I'll name it with the cue numbers and names that are used within each track. I now have my first pass of an album that's ready to present to the client. It's time to export each track and send for feedback. Here's what a finished sequence might look like:

Part Five
File Delivery

Once the soundtrack album is ready to send to the client(s) for feedback, it's time to export each track as a standalone audio file. Since we're listening for content, not audio quality, I usually create MP3s of each track just to keep file sizes small, and they hold metadata that is helpful.

I export each track individually and name it with the shorthand version of the project's name. Often this is just the initials of the name of the show, or a shortened version of the name. To give a few examples from my own experience, *Training Day* was "TD," *Hitchcock* was "Hitch", and *Stargirl* was "SGL." I then indicate the track number followed by the track name. Sometimes I'll use the cue number(s) of the cue(s) being used within the track followed by the name of the track. Most often the name of the track will match the name of the cue being used, but not always. This is especially common when using multiple cues to create a single track, I'll either use the name of one of the cues or perhaps come up with a new name that is evocative of something appropriate from the film/show. When I scored *Jasmine*, the first piece I wrote was a demo of what would become Jasmine's theme and establish a tone for the movie. The cue wasn't written to picture and never made it into the film. When releasing the soundtrack album, the director & I decided to include it as the final track of the album and simply named it "Jasmine's Theme."

Using *My Awesome Movie* as an example, and simply using "Track 1, Track 2, Track 3," etc. as track names, filenames would look something like this:

MAM 01 1m01 v3 ALT & 2m22 v1 Track 1 v1 or MAM 01 Track 1

MAM 02 1m03 v2 & 2m26v1 Track 2 v1   or MAM 02 Track 2

MAM 03 1m09 v2 Track 3 v1   or MAM 03 Track 3

MAM 04 3m47B v2 Track 4 v2   or MAM 04 Track 4

MAM 05 1m11 v2 & 2m30 v1 Track 5 v1   or MAM 05 Track 5

Etc.

In the metadata of the MP3 file I'll have the title to match the filename, add the composer's name in the Artist field, put in the project name + "Soundtrack" and the version number in the Album field, and "NOT FOR DISTRIBUTION" in the Comment field to make sure it is clear this file is not meant to be shared with anyone in the public. Finally, I'll select Soundtrack for the Genre field, type in the track number and the year in the corresponding fields and export. Using Pro Tools it'll look like the image below, other DAWs have a similar window where you can enter this metadata, or you can edit the metadata after exporting using any number of available meta-tagging tools:

MP3

Encoder

Mac File

Encoding Quality: Highest

Type: MPG3   Creator: mAmp

Constant Bit Rate (CBR): 128kbit/s

ID3 Tag Info

Tag Type: ID3 v2.3

Title: MAM 01 1m01 v3 ALT & 2m22v1 Track v1

Artist: Awesome Composer

Album: My Awesome Movie Soundtrack v1

Comment: NOT FOR DISTRIBUTION

Genre: Soundtrack

Track: 1   Year: 2026

Defaults   Cancel   OK

Once the client(s) have sent me any notes I'll address those and then export the new versions, which would be the same as above, but have v2 at the end of each track name. Usually most tracks remain unchanged, so Track 3 v1 & v2 might be identical. I'm keeping track of the soundtrack version, not the individual track version. Whether the track is the same or different isn't important in this case, because what matters is the entire album, and I want it to be crystal clear for the client that this is the track that is part of whichever version of the soundtrack album I'm on.

In my experience I will usually have 1 or 2 rounds of notes from the client(s), incrementing the version number with each round. Once the soundtrack is approved it's time to send it off to mastering.

Part Six
Mastering

If you're reading this booklet, I assume you're familiar with the process of mastering. But just in case here's my quick explanation of what this process is. It is the final polish applied to the audio to make sure that the music really shines in its intended release format. Mastering for a digital streaming release might be different than mastering for a physical release, especially on vinyl. I like to compare the process of mastering to color correction, where the image is tweaked to make sure the contrast, color balance, and hues are all just right. Of course what's just right is a creative decision, one might want an image to look a little more red or a little more blue, a little darker or lighter, more contrast or less — all subjective choices.

Photo courtesy of Maor Appelbaum Mastering.

The same is true for audio mastering, there are creative choices to be made that are entirely subjective. However, there are also some technical guidelines that are addressed during this process, especially relating to loudness. You don't want your listeners reaching for the volume dial when your album comes on following someone else's album, nor do you want them reaching for it when listening from one track to the next.

Finding the right mastering engineer is important. It's like finding the right musician for a performance or the right orchestrator for your work. Presumably all mastering engineers know what they're doing technically and will do a fine job, but they each bring their own unique perspective, creative approach, experience and personality to their work. Some people like to be at the mastering session and in the room with the mastering engineer giving notes in real time. Some prefer to let the mastering engineer do their work on their own, receive hi-resolution WAV files to review in the comfort of their own studio and then give notes. Some mastering engineers relish having the client at the sessions with them, others prefer to work alone. Like all other things in the creative field, you want to find the right fit for you and your project.

A mastering engineer that specializes in pop albums might not be the best choice to master an orchestral soundtrack. On the other hand, they might be ideal to master a pop influenced score and be a better fit than someone who specializes in orchestral music. Conversely, just because they primarily work in one genre of music doesn't mean they can't be great at working in other genres of music. In some instances, they may even bring a unique approach that is fresh and exciting. Some have lots of experience mastering for vinyl, others might not. So, depending on what you're looking for, different people might be the best fit for you and your soundtrack album. I don't like to pigeonhole anyone and tend to work with the same mastering engineer over and over when the choice is in my hands. Though on occasion I'll use someone else, either because the client wants someone else, or perhaps the studio or record label is paying for the album and they have their preferred mastering engineers, or perhaps due to availability or affordability. Whatever the case, find someone that you feel good about and trust them, their instincts, their creativity and their skill to do a great job for you. And don't be afraid to ask lots of questions when looking for the right mastering engineer. It's an important decision and you should be comfortable with it.

When sending an album to mastering, I always check in with the engineer to discuss their preferred method of receiving the materials. Often, they're very happy to get a Pro Tools session where they can see all the edits, and if there are stems, they have all those stems to work with. My most common delivery method is sending my Pro Tools session, in which case I'll do a "Save Session Copy in..." and add "to mastering" to the end of the filename. I only export the tracks they need, typically just "MX A" and "MX B," as described earlier in this booklet. They don't need the track containing everything or all my trimmed edits, they just need what's on the album. Here's what that looks like once again.

Some mastering engineers don't use Pro Tools and prefer to receive individual files that they can import into the DAW of their choice. If that's the case I'll bounce each track as described earlier when sending for client review, but instead of making MP3s I'll create hi-resolution WAV files. I always check with the mastering engineer regarding their specs for sample rate and bit depth.

Usually, they want the highest specs available. Most commonly in film-scoring that's 48 kHz, 24 Bit and so I'll export WAV files at those specs and clearly name them as described earlier. If I have stems and they want them, but they are requesting individual audio files, I'll export each stem as its own WAV file making sure they all start and end at the exact same place and are all clearly labeled by adding the name of the stem at the end of the filename. For example, MAM 01 Track 1 - Strings.

Once the mastering engineer sends the mastered tracks back to me, I'll send them to the client to review and also listen to them myself. I jot down any notes I might have and hang on to them until I get the client notes, if any. It's quite common for the client to have similar notes to mine, in which case I have nothing to add. But if I do have something to add or suggest, I'll run it by the client and see if they agree with the note. I then collate all the notes into a single email and send them to the mastering engineer to address.

In my experience it's pretty rare that we need more than a single round of notes, though on occasion there might be a second or even third round of notes, especially if there are several people offering feedback. Once the mastering is approved, I will connect the mastering engineer with the appropriate person at the record label or studio so they can directly deliver the mastered tracks directly to them for distribution. If there is no record label or studio involved and the album will be self-released, then the final mastered files are delivered to me to either pass on to the client or to upload them to the distributor of their choice on their behalf (i.e. DistroKid, Songtrdr, CD Baby, etc.).

- 42 -

Part Seven
Credits, Paperwork, and Artwork

Part of my job when creating a soundtrack album is collecting all the credits for the record label and/or studio and filling out paperwork to provide them with all the information they need. This information is used to enter metadata for digital releases, album credits on physical releases, and to properly distribute any royalty payments that may be due to composers and/or artists. Here is a list of the information they typically require for each album:

- Album Name.
- Album Artist.
- Album Producer(s).
- Album Executive Music Producer(s), if any.
- Music Supervisor, if there was one on the project.
- Score Mixer(s).
- Music Editor(s).

- Mastering Engineer(s).
- Orchestrator(s).
- Music Preparation.
- Conductor(s).
- Score Coordinator.
- Where the score was recorded, meaning the name of the studio, for example "Budapest Scoring" or "The Barbara Streisand Scoring Stage."
- Orchestral Arrangements, if relevant.
- Vocal Contractor, if relevant.
- Musician Contractor, if relevant.
- Vocal Ensemble, if relevant.
- Additional Music by credits.
- Recording Engineer.
- Where the score was mixed, again meaning the studio, for example "Hollywood Scoring" or "Capitol Studios."
- Assistants, this can include the composer's assistant(s), assistant engineers, assistant orchestrators, assistant contractors...
- Thank Yous, this is an opportunity for the composer to include any thank yous they may have.

In addition, here is a list of all the data they typically require for each track:

- Track Number.
- Track Title.
- Display Artist(s), this is what appears in the metadata on the streaming services, or is embedded into CDs if those are still used.
- Duration.

- Cue numbers, I typically get this request from studios who like to know what makes up each track. Record labels won't usually ask for this.
- Composer(s).
- Composer(s) PRO, i.e. ASCAP, BMI, etc.
- Composer(s) splits, if there is more than one composer this is the percentage share of the composition for each composer.
- Publisher(s).
- Publisher(s) splits, if there is more than one publisher.
- Recording Country.
- Producer(s).
- Mastering Engineer.
- Lyrics, if relevant.

The composer/publisher information is the same as what is required for cue sheets, so if you're acquainted with those, this will be very familiar, too. Sometimes they'll also ask for the mixing engineer's name per track, the Artist Spotify profile link, the Artist Apple profile link, artist social media handles, and a list of any additional performers for each track (for example the names of SAG vocalists if any, or other soloists).

Usually whomever requires this information will either have a google sheet or some other template available that they'll want you to use to provide all the above information.

When working with a record label on a physical release it's quite common for them to want the track listing ASAP. I've even had instances where they asked me to simply inform them of approximately how many tracks I expect will be on the album even if it's not done yet. The reason is that they need their graphic artists to work on the graphic design for the physical release and knowing approximately how many tracks the album will have allows them to work on a design even if they don't yet have the exact number or even all the track names. They use placeholders for that.

Speaking of artwork, when working with a studio or record label, they will have people to handle all of that and usually neither I nor the composer have any say in the matter. Sometimes they may share mockups with us as a courtesy or even and ask for our opinion when they have several options they are considering. But often we're completely out of the graphic art loop.

When working on independent films that don't have a studio behind them it's far more common for me to be involved in this part of the album too. If it's a self-release, then it's up to me to handle the artwork. In such cases I'll usually coordinate with the project's director and/or producer who can usually provide hi-res still images from the film, including a version of the poster that can be used to create the album artwork. Sometimes they can provide the artwork at the proper specs for an album because they either have the skill and tools to create them themselves, or they have a graphic artist that can do it for them. This was the case in a recent soundtrack album of my own score to Joe Ferro's short film *Compound Machines*.

On self-releases of my own albums, or for friends that I've helped, I've hired freelance graphic artists to help. On occasion I even created my own album cover art using Photoshop. These days there are also AI tools that can help, though I prefer to work with human beings and find a graphic artist that can create a design for me. Keep in mind that when creating your own soundtrack albums of your own music for self-releases you'll be responsible for the artwork too.

Addendum One
Vinyl Albums

When working on albums that will be released on vinyl, there are a few special considerations to keep in mind due to the physical nature of how vinyl albums are made. Vinyl albums are made by etching grooves into a round disc, with each side of the disc containing its own set of grooves. The first track on each side is on the outside of the disc, the last on the inside. As a vinyl record plays, the needle moves from the outer edge toward the center, traveling across grooves with progressively smaller diameters. This decreasing circumference creates physical limitations: less surface area per revolution, reduced groove definition and tighter spacing between grooves. The result is diminished fidelity, compromised clarity, and increased risk of "kissing grooves" (adjacent grooves touching) that cause needle skips. These physical constraints lead to more limited dynamic range and often brittle sound quality as the needle approaches the inner portions of the disc.

To preserve optimal sound quality, consider these guidelines for side lengths:

- 18-20 minutes or less per side is ideal for most music.
- For soundtracks or less loud/compressed music, up to 22 minutes works well..
- Exceeding 25 minutes significantly compromises overall sound quality.

When longer side lengths are unavoidable, several strategies can minimize quality loss. While keeping overall volume more modest helps accommodate additional music, the most effective approach is strategic sequencing. Place louder, more energetic tracks earlier on each side, reserving quieter, less compressed material for the innermost grooves. These quieter, more relaxed tracks can maintain better fidelity in the physically constrained inner diameter where louder, more intense tracks would suffer noticeable degradation.

When I created the digital and vinyl versions of Pinar Toprak's soundtrack albums for *Avatar: Frontiers of Pandora*, I sequenced each version differently for the reasons described above. In the digital version we started with a track called "The People's Cry (Main Theme)" which is a beautiful, soulful and quiet track. The second track "Take Flight" is an exciting loud track, and the third track "Child of Two Worlds" begins quite softly, builds and then comes back down again. Opening with these three tracks in this order makes for a compelling listen, and introduces themes from the soundtrack, which is why we chose it for the digital album.

In order to maximize how many minutes we could fit on the vinyl album, that version begins with "Child of Two Worlds," which has a pretty large dynamic range. Then the second track is "Take Flight" like on the digital album, still near the outside of the disc where we can maximize the loudness and dynamic range of this exciting cue, and then the third track is "The Sarentu Moot," which is track 6 on the digital version. We had to eliminate tracks 4 & 5 of the digital album because the double vinyl album couldn't fit as much music. The final track on side 1 of the vinyl album is "Glade of Light," a relatively quiet cue with a limited dynamic range. This same track appears as track 36 on the digital version.

As you can see, I had to make specific choices to make sure the vinyl version also provides a very engaging listening experience in its own unique way, while maximizing the physical limitations of vinyl. And in case you're wondering, "The People's Cry (Main Theme)" which opens the digital album is the final track on side 4 of the double vinyl album.

We made similar choices when creating the digital and vinyl versions of the soundtrack to *Slumberland*. In that one the biggest change was keeping the final cue of the film which was written for the Main on Ends as the final cue of the digital soundtrack. But since it's a very exciting and loud cue, we opted to make it the very first cue on the vinyl version.

There are also unique considerations when it comes to mastering vinyl albums. This goes beyond my personal expertise, so I can't really offer much in terms of details, but the technical specifications differ from those of digital-only albums. Additionally, the physical limitations I described above also affect the mastering process and how loud an album can be overall. Ideally a digital album would be mastered independently of the vinyl version to make the most of each format. However, that's an expensive endeavor, and so often it's mastered for digital release, and then a global level adjustment might be made when creating the master plate for pressing the vinyl albums.

If you're interested in learning more about vinyl mastering, Jett Galindo has a wonderful article on the subject which can be found at https://www.izotope.com/en/learn/mastering-for-vinyl-tips-for-digital-mastering-engineers.html

- 54 -

Addendum Two
Mixed Score & Song Albums

When creating albums that combine score and songs there are some considerations to keep in mind when determining the sequence of the tracks. In my opinion interspersing songs and score doesn't usually work very well. I feel it breaks up the score, makes the album feel choppy, and can be tricky when mastering since the dynamic range of songs and score are often very different. My recommendation is to either have the songs appear one after the other at the beginning of the album, before the score tracks, or do the reverse. Start with the score, and then include the songs at the end.

That said, there are examples of soundtracks that don't follow this advice. The soundtrack album to *Apollo 13* (score by James Horner) is an example that intersperses score and songs along with some audio clips from the film. This album was designed before streaming at a time when vinyl wasn't popular and CDs were the format of choice. With CDs we were able to have music play continuously and insert a track index anywhere we wanted. So, we could have tracks segue from one to another seamlessly when listening in order, or one could skip to whichever track one wanted. This doesn't work in streaming and there will always be a brief moment of silence between tracks. It's only a fraction of a second, but it breaks the continuity of the audio and so sequencing albums like this has fallen out of fashion.

I noticed many of Thomas Newman's soundtrack albums mix songs and score and generally tend to sequence things in show order, so songs are interspersed with score. While I'm a huge fan of his music, it always bumps me when listening to his soundtracks when a song appears in the middle of the score. As I said in the introduction, there is no right or wrong way and all I can do is share my opinions and process.

Below are a couple of real-world examples from albums I worked on that included both songs and score and how we approached them.

When I worked on Danny Elfman's soundtrack album to *Big Fish* there was the score, an original song by Pearl Jam written for the end credits of the film, a handful of licensed songs that were featured in the film and in addition Danny had written an original song that was performed within the film that we wanted to include on the album. The solution we came up with was to start with the original Pearl Jam song "Man Of the Hour" followed by the licensed songs, which made up tracks 2-7. Tracks 8-22 were all score, followed by Danny's original song "Twice the Love (Siamese Twins' Song)" to close out the album. I remember we tried having Danny's song with the other songs, but it didn't feel like it was the right fit. We tried having the songs at the end, but ultimately, we felt starting with the songs and ending with Danny's music was the better approach, which created a logical and engaging listening experience that worked well. This album was also designed when CDs were the primary format, but unlike the *Apollo 13* example I gave above, we didn't have any tracks that segue from one to another so it works just as well on streaming platforms today as it did on CD.

On Pinar Toprak's soundtrack to *The Lost City (Music from the Motion Picture)*, we had the score, an original arrangement of Europe's hit "The Final Countdown" that mixed a recreation of the original synths, drums and guitars with full orchestra, and three songs that were used within the movie. We ended up starting with the score, followed by "The Final Countdown," then the three songs, and finally we decided to add a couple of bonus tracks that were original music by Pinar, but they didn't really fit in with the rest of the score. One was a quirky one-off cue that everyone loved and wanted to include, the other was a source cue written for the film. This album was designed to be digital only, so we didn't need to think about any physical limitations that would come into play as described in the previous chapter had it also been released on vinyl.

- 58 -

Addendum Three
Live Theater Soundtrack Albums

There is one more type of soundtrack album that hasn't been addressed in this book, and that is live theater soundtrack albums. There are two types of these albums that I can think of. One is a studio recording of a stage musical, where the cast and musicians record all the songs in a studio environment. The other is a live recording of a performance (or several performances). These kinds of soundtrack albums present a few unique challenges and considerations that we do not see in film, TV or videogame soundtracks.

The first key difference is that when we're working with a film or TV or videogame score, the music has been written, recorded, mixed and delivered and we're either working with the full mix or mix stems. However, with these types of albums, most if not all of the creative editorial choices are made before the music is mixed.

In the case of a studio recording, sometimes we have slightly different arrangements than those that are performed live on stage. The studio environment allows for production techniques that a live performance might not, and so when creating such an album the first question is should the recording perfectly replicate a live recording? Or should adjustments be made to take advantage of what's possible in the studio. Adjustments could include changes to the song structure because there might be dialog bits or engaging choreography in the live show that are trimmed or for the album as the music might not be quite as thrilling for as long absent these other elements. Other adjustments could be the orchestra/band size. Hiring a 40- or 50-piece orchestra every night for a live performance on Broadway may not be economically viable or practical. Certain venues might not be able to fit such a large group, but one might decide to have a larger size orchestra for a one-time studio recording.

Studio recordings also enable overdubbing, so one might opt to overdub guitars to beef up the sound or add more elements to the arrangement that don't exist in the live show, which might only have a single guitarist performing. The same is applicable to any instrument. Studio recordings also allow for recording techniques that might not be possible in a live show, such as individually striping different instruments or sections, and complete sonic separation between instruments that is impossible in a live show where there will almost always be some mic-bleed. And finally in a studio environment one can record take after take and comp the best possible performance together, much like when working on a film or TV or videogame score, which obviously isn't the case in a live performance. This can afford a studio recording a lot more control than when working with a live recording.

Other considerations that can come into play are conceptual approaches of how to record such an album. Should the entire band/orchestra perform simultaneously with the entire cast? Should the band be recorded separately from the orchestra, and then have the cast come in to record the vocals later? If opting for the former, will the studio recording endeavor to capture a performance just like a live show but in a studio setting? Or will there be starts and stop to do additional takes? Will the music be performed exactly as in the show, or will there be any editorial changes to the structure of the songs for creative reasons. For example, in a live show there may be some dialog within a song that might be omitted from the studio album version. A stage production may have highly choreographed numbers or other visuals that allow for expanded arrangements, but absent those visual elements it might make more sense to shorten certain sections of a song for the purposes of a soundtrack album.

These are all choices that must be considered and made as part of the recording process for this type of album. Though some of these choices, like shortening a particular section, could still happen after the mix just like when working on a film score soundtrack album.

In the case of a live recording, one would almost have to get involved in the album production process before the music is even mixed as it would be impossible to make some decisions after the mix. There is lots of cleanup that must be done on live recordings to prepare them for a proper mix. If there are multiple recordings from multiple performances, there are choices to be made of which performance is best, or which parts of each recording is best and what kind of comping is or isn't possible to produce the best possible result. Live performances can include mistakes, or one-off executions that may either be desirable or undesirable, so creative choices have to be made when comping the materials for the mix that are impossible to make after the mix is done. This is like comping different takes when recording a film cue, which happens long before we start working on a soundtrack album.

Live recordings will have some audio bleed in different microphones, so one may or may not be able to completely remove the sound of applause. This raises the question, is the approach to try and minimize the audience in the recording? Or perhaps to embrace it and feature it where appropriate?

It's not uncommon for the cast to wait for applause to subside before moving on to the next song, does one leave the full duration of the applause in the soundtrack album? Or does one trim it? In a comedic musical, there may be improvised jokes that happen on stage. Does one keep those in the album? Or should they be trimmed and omitted so the soundtrack focuses entirely on the songs? Similarly, there may be non-singing reactions, callouts, or dialog within a song, do we want to keep that in the soundtrack album? Or omit it?

These are all unique considerations when working on live-theater albums, and unlike a film or TV soundtrack album, where creative choices are made after the score has been mixed and delivered, here many, if not most choices must be made earlier in the process.

- 64 -

Final Thoughts

There are a few more unusual scenarios that I didn't discuss but I want to mention. Some soundtrack albums incorporate some dialog or even sound effects from the film. The soundtrack album to *Apollo 13*, which I mentioned earlier is one example. In that album short clips of audio were interspersed between songs and score. The very first thing we hear on the soundtrack album to *Meet Joe Black* is Brad Pitt's voice saying "yes." The soundtrack to *Reservoir Dogs* includes snippets of dialog that are about a minute long between some of the music tracks. These are just a few examples.

I think I get what they were trying to do, but honestly, I don't love it. For me a soundtrack album is about the music. It's a way to highlight the score and/or songs away from the movie and I find dialog snippets detract from this, especially if they are on top of the music, which is sometimes the case.

In the previous chapter I mentioned bonus tracks on Pinar Toprak's album to *The Lost City*. On occasion there might be one or two cues that are one-offs, they're not in the style of the rest of the score and as a listening experience they don't really fit well within the sequencing of the rest of the score. But they may be really cool and well worth including in a soundtrack. A great solution is putting them at the end of the album and calling the bonus tracks. Having them at the end ensures they don't feel out of place within the listening experience of the rest of the score and being labeled as bonus tracks differentiates them from the rest of the score. It makes the album feel like it ended with the last non bonus track, and now we have a little extra gift.

The *Mass Effect* video game series have quite a few soundtrack albums for the various iterations of the game. They even created an EP specifically for bonus tracks called *Mass Effect: Trilogy Collection Bonus Tracks*. I think this is a really cool idea, but only works on a franchise where there are already multiple soundtracks.

Finally, another fun surprise can be hidden tracks. Hidden tracks are typically an extra track at the very end of the album that doesn't appear in the track listing and doesn't have its own track number. The final listed track ends and after a brief pause the hidden track plays. They are most commonly found on pop albums. I rarely see these in soundtracks, but one example that comes to mind is in Danny Elfman's *The Nightmare Before Christmas: Original Motion Picture Soundtrack* there was a hidden track on the original CD version on the final track. Track 20 "End Credits" on the original CD version was 5:05 long, while on the digital streaming version the hidden track appears to have been removed, and it is just 3:52 long. If you have a short reprise that you really love, or some one-off cue that doesn't really fit within the body of your album, making it a hidden track can be a fun surprise for fans.

As I see it, soundtrack albums are a way to highlight the music from films, TV shows and videogames outside of the projects for which they were created. They are a treat for fans who have the opportunity to enjoy the music on its own. And because they stand on their own, they don't have to be exact matches of the way they appeared in the production, nor is it necessary to hear them in the order in which they appeared. Quite the contrary, more often than not, editing some cues to shorten them, or as I described "trim the fat," combining cues that weren't originally connected, or even extending cues can make for a more enjoyable album. And that's what it's all about, making sure that the audience has the best possible listening experience.

I hope this booklet provides some valuable insights and methods to help you make the best possible soundtrack album you can. Remember, there are no rules, no right or wrong way to go about it, just choices to be made. Don't get hung up on keeping things as close to the way they were in the production. Move things around, experiment, try out ideas and see how they feel. At the end of the day if you love listening to the album as you created it, chances are so will fans.

About the Author

Composer and music editor Shie Rozow (pronounced shy ro-zov) has taken a different path than most leading him to work on over 150 feature films including major international blockbusters like Paw Patrol: The Mighty Movie, Avengers: Age of Ultron, Guardians of the Galaxy, Hustle & Flow and Training Day.

Armed with over 25 years of industry experience and driven by his lifelong passion for music and storytelling, Shie has earned 17 Golden Reel Award Nominations, winning for his work on *Chicago* (as assistant music editor), *IMAX: Deep Sea*, and *Wu Tang: An American Saga*. He brings his inexhaustible talent and natural ear for music to every story, weaving a rich musical narrative that compliments the filmmaker's vision and unlocks new layers of depth.

Equally skilled working in film, TV, and video games, Shie has contributed his talent on hundreds of hours of TV including *Desperate Housewives, Arrow,* and most recently The CW's *Stargirl,* along with Amazon's anthology series *Welcome to the Blumhouse* and Shudder's *Creepshow.* Shie produced the Grammy Nominated score to *Avatar: Frontiers of Pandora* and has also worked on music for *Disney* theme parks, *Cirque du Soleil* and the 2025 Hollywood Bowl production of *Jesus Christ Superstar* starring Cynthia Erivo and Adam Lambert. Shie also composes concert music, which has been performed from coast to coast, releasing his first album *Musical Fantasy* in 2016.

You can hear his music on Netflix's documentary *Shawn Mendes: In Wonder* as well as award-winning indie features like *Jasmine, Camp Arrowhead, Captain Hagen's Bed and Breakfast,* and the feature documentary *The Last of the Winthrops.* His scores to *Matt and Maya, Lost Time, One Day You'll Go Blind, Body Language: Bill Shannon,* and *Granville & Georgia: 150 Years in VR* have all won Telly Awards.

Shie's first book, "Preparing for Scoring Sessions", was published in March 2023, reaching number one on Amazon. His second book "Every Note Tells a Story", aims to distil his professional experience into a concise, cohesive and practical handbook that inspires filmmakers, composers and fans with a deep appreciation for the film scoring process. The book won multiple awards including the Pencraft Award for Literary Excellence, the Literary Global Book

Award, and Best Indie Book Award.

A graduate of Berklee College of Music, where he completed his 4-year degree in just 5 semesters, ("being broke is a great incentive," he explained), Shie lives in Los Angeles with his wife, two children, and their many pets. He enjoys photography, astronomy and SCUBA diving in his free time.

To learn more about Shie and his work, visit his website at www.shierozow.com.

The Art and Craft of Creating Engaging Soundtrack Albums

More Books in This Series
Preparing for Scoring Sessions

A detailed guide to preparing to record music for media (film/ TV/games) covering everything from organization, budgeting and scheduling to large scale scoring sessions, small scale remote recordings, material preparation and more. This guide covers technical, creative and practical considerations along with tips and examples based on the author's 25 years of experience in the industry working on projects ranging from low budget independent short films, to some of the biggest blockbusters Hollywood has produced.

- 74 -